GREAT CITIES
OF THE WORLD

ST. PETERSBURG

ANDREW LAN

WORLD ALMANAC® LIBRARY

Please visit our web site at: www.worldalmanaclibrary.com
For a free color catalog describing World Almanac® Library's list of high-quality books
and multimedia programs, call 1-800-848-2928 (USA) or 1-800-387-3178 (Canada).
World Almanac® Library's fax: (414) 332-3567.

Library of Congress Cataloging-in-Publication Data

Langley, Andrew.
    St. Petersburg / by Andrew Langley.
       p. cm. — (Great cities of the world)
    Includes bibliographical references and index.
    ISBN 0-8368-5054-8 (lib. bdg.)
    ISBN 0-8368-5214-1 (softcover)
    1. Saint Petersburg (Russia)—Juvenile literature. I. Title. II. Series.
    DK552.L33 2005
    947'.21—dc22   2005042589

First published in 2006 by
World Almanac® Library
A Member of the WRC Media Family of Companies
330 West Olive Street, Suite 100
Milwaukee, WI 53212 USA

Produced by Discovery Books
Editors: Betsy Rasmussen and Helen Dwyer
Series designers: Laurie Shock, Keith Williams
Designer and page production: Keith Williams
Photo researcher: Rachel Tisdale
Maps: Stefan Chabluk
World Almanac® Library editorial direction: Mark J. Sachner
World Almanac® Library editor: Gini Holland
World Almanac® Library art direction: Tammy West
World Almanac® Library graphic design: Scott M. Krall
World Almanac® Library production: Jessica Morris

Photo credits: AKG Images: pp.12, 18; AKG Images/Ullstein: p.35; Art Directors & Trip/Flora Torrance: p.20; Art Directors &
Trip/Martin Barlow: p.26; Art Directors & Trip/Tibor Bognar: p.40; Corbis/Antoine Gyori: p.25; Corbis/Antoine Gyori/Sygma:
p.32; Corbis/Bob Krist: p.38; Corbis/Jason Reed/Reuters: p.42; Corbis/Rose Hartman: p.28; Corbis/Steve Raymer: pp.16, 24;
Corbis/Wolfgang Kaehler: p.41; Getty Images: p.8; Getty Images/Erica Lansner: p.22; Getty Images/John Lamb/Stone: p.11;
Getty Images/Scott Peterson: p.30; Getty Images/Sergei Supinsky/AFP: p.15; Getty Images/STR/AFP: p.39; Sovphoto: p.14;
Sovphoto/TASS: pp. 4, 7, 29, 33, 36, 43; Still Pictures/Annelies van Brink: p.23.

Cover: The Neva River runs through the heart of St. Petersburg (photograph reproduced by permission of
Sovphoto/TASS).

Printed in Canada

1 2 3 4 5 6 7 8 9 09 08 07 06 05

Contents

Introduction

St. Petersburg is a relatively young Eastern European city, founded only three centuries ago in 1703. The city's name has changed more than once as Russian political fortunes changed: from St. Petersburg to Petrograd to Leningrad and finally back to St. Petersburg. Today, St. Petersburg is the second-largest city in the Russian Federation (after Moscow) with the fourth-highest population of any city in

◀ *Palace Square has been the scene of many crucial moments in St. Petersburg's history. Today, it is still used for public meetings and rock concerts.*

Europe. It forms an important industrial center and a major junction for air, rail, and water transportation.

Watery Window on the West

The Russian Federation, or Russia, is the largest country in the world, stretching from the borders of Europe in the west across to the Pacific Coast in the Asian east. St. Petersburg stands at the northwest corner of this vast land on the Gulf of Finland, which leads into the Baltic Sea. On the threshold of Europe, St. Petersburg is known as Russia's "Window on the West."

The city is also called the "Venice of the North." Like the famous Italian city of Venice, St. Petersburg contains large areas of water. It is built on the marshy, low-lying land at the delta of the Neva River and is crisscrossed by canals and many other waterways. Buildings in the city stand on land that is at no point more than 13 feet (4 meters) above sea level.

City Overview

St. Petersburg is flat with no hills nearby. The best way to get a view of the city is to climb almost three hundred steps to the colonnade that runs around the outside of the vast dome of St. Isaac's Cathedral, the largest cathedral in St. Petersburg. Seen from here, the layout of this great city becomes clear.

The most obvious geographical feature of the city is the wide Neva River that splits into two branches, the Big Neva and the Little Neva. These waterways divide

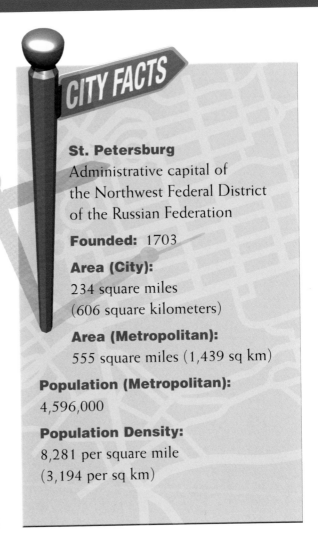

CITY FACTS

St. Petersburg
Administrative capital of the Northwest Federal District of the Russian Federation

Founded: 1703

Area (City):
234 square miles
(606 square kilometers)

Area (Metropolitan):
555 square miles (1,439 sq km)

Population (Metropolitan):
4,596,000

Population Density:
8,281 per square mile
(3,194 per sq km)

St. Petersburg into sections. The section located on the south bank is the largest. It is lined with large and important buildings, including the Winter Palace (a former residence for Russian czars), the Admiralty (a naval college), and St. Isaac's Cathedral. It also contains shopping and commercial buildings. Across the river to the west is Vasilevsky Island, St. Petersburg's largest island and home to the city's university and many museums. A sprawl of suburbs surrounds the city to complete the St. Petersburg metropolitan area.

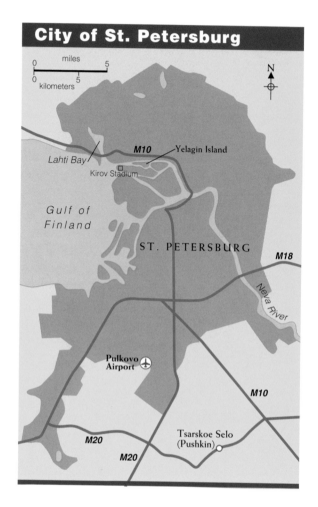

City of St. Petersburg

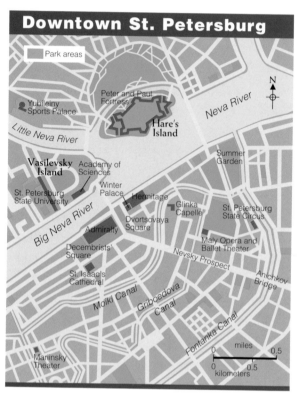

Downtown St. Petersburg

Climate

St. Petersburg lies about only 500 miles (800 kilometers) from the Arctic Circle, but it has a surprisingly mild climate because it is warmed by sea currents. The marine air brings with it a lot of moisture and wind. Periods of mist and heavy cloud cover are frequent, and the area has high annual precipitation.

Spring begins in March and is usually cool. By June, when summer starts, the weather is often warm and dry. The days become crisper by September, and the first snow usually appears in October.

During the winter, temperatures gradually drop to below freezing, and from January to March heavy snowfall occurs. The waterways, including the Neva River and the harbor, are mostly frozen over between November and April.

Because St. Petersburg is so far north, the city has long nights in winter and long days in summer. By late June, the Sun barely sets, and it stays light for almost the entire twenty-four hours of each day. In midwinter, the days are very dark, with less than one hour of sunlight.

Cultural Capital

St. Petersburg has been at the center of Russia's artistic life since its founding. It

Built on Water

Water is never far away in St. Petersburg. Ten percent of the city's area consists of water. Forty waterways snake for a total distance of 135 miles (217 km). Crossed by at least 580 bridges, the waterways are home to more than forty islands. During the three hundred years since its founding, St. Petersburg has flooded 288 times.

▲ *The Neva River runs through the heart of the city and is crossed by several fine bridges. The dome of St. Isaac's Cathedral can be seen in the background.*

contains beautiful architecture and is home to some of the greatest works of art in the world, most notably the collections in the Hermitage Museum, which contain masterpieces by many great artists.

Many of Russia's greatest writers and composers lived in St. Petersburg, including Alexander Pushkin, Fyodor Dostoyevsky, Anna Akhmatova, and Peter Ilyich Tchaikovsky, and much of their work is closely connected with the city. The St. Petersburg School of Ballet has produced many legendary stars, such as Anna Pavlova and Vaslav Nijinsky, and the world-famous Kirov Ballet Company is still based at the Mariinsky Theater.

"St. Petersburg …
the brother of water and sky."

—Osip Mandelstam, Russian poet, 1928.

CHAPTER 1

History of St. Petersburg

Most great cities began as small settlements and grew gradually over many centuries. St. Petersburg's growth was different, however. It was created at great speed by the determination of one man—Peter the Great, czar (emperor) of Russia.

Victory over Sweden

The mouth of the Neva River was not an inviting place to found a city in the early eighteenth century. Marshy and flat, the land was plagued with mosquitoes in summer and floods in winter. The only people who visited this damp, desolate spot were fishers and hunters.

"The sense of something glorious but something not stable on its feet. . . . I think the fact that the city is built on a swamp really has an effect on that— the sense that the whole city could disappear in a second."

—Ingrid Bengis, Russian/American writer living in St. Petersburg, 2003

◄ *Peter the Great, architect of the Russian nation and founder of St. Petersburg.*

When Peter became ruler of Russia in 1689, however, he decided this area was the perfect site for his new capital city because it would give him access to the Baltic Sea, which was vital for trade with Europe. His first step toward this goal was to capture the territory from the neighboring country of Sweden. In 1700, he began a twenty-year war against Sweden to gain power over the Baltic Sea routes, and he soon drove the Swedes from the Neva delta.

On May 16, 1703, Peter landed on Hare's Island, one of the many islands on the north side of the Neva River. He cut two strips of turf with his bayonet and laid one across the other so that it formed an X. "Here there shall be a town," he said. His workers began building the Peter and Paul Fortress and a wooden hut on a neighboring island for Peter to live in temporarily. He named the city after his patron saint, Peter. A victory over the Swedes at Poltava (in Ukraine) in 1709 ensured that the region would remain Russian, even though the war continued for many more years.

Building a Capital

Creating a city in this marshy wilderness was a backbreaking challenge. All the stone and other building materials had to be transported from far away. Thousands of wooden "piles" (heavy beams) had to be hammered into the boggy ground to make firm foundations for the heavy buildings. Vast armies of peasants and Swedish prisoners of war dug and cut and carried the

"Now indeed with God's help the final stone has been laid in the foundation of St. Petersburg."

—Peter the Great, after his victory over the Swedish army at Poltava in 1709.

building materials. Countless numbers of workers died there, and it is said that St. Petersburg is built on their bones.

Peter worked his labor force ruthlessly. Canals were dug to drain the marshes; two new royal palaces were built (one for winter, one for summer); and soon the city stretched along both banks of the Neva River. In 1712, St. Petersburg became Russia's new capital. Peter moved his nobles and officials to St. Petersburg from Moscow and forced them to erect extravagant new homes. When Peter died in 1725, the population of the new city had risen to more than forty thousand.

The Golden Age of St. Petersburg

For a few years, Peter's great city had to take second place because Russia's new ruler moved the capital back to Moscow. In 1741, however, the royal court returned to St. Petersburg, and the city began to grow again. Under the Empresses Elizabeth and Catherine II (the Great), more new architecture was commissioned. Each hired architects from Western Europe to design palaces, bridges, and official buildings in the classical style.

Two Greats

Peter the Great (1672–1725)

Huge, strong-willed, and dynamic, Peter the Great transformed Russia from a backward nation into a great world power. He saw that Russia's future lay in copying the successful countries of Western Europe, which he toured in 1697–1698. So he built St. Petersburg, a brand-new capital city with easier access to Europe's trade routes. He also improved the Russian civil service and army, and he formed its first real navy. He encouraged his people to follow Western customs, even forcing men to shave off their old-fashioned beards.

Catherine the Great (1729–1796)

At the age of fifteen, Catherine left her home in Prussia (a former kingdom that included parts of Germany) and went to St. Petersburg to marry the heir to the throne of Russia. Her husband, however, turned out to be a feeble ruler. In 1762, he was assassinated, and Catherine took his place. As empress of Russia, she carried on the work of Peter the Great with enormous energy, expanding Russian power in the West and south and modernizing industry and education.

Catherine also made St. Petersburg a center of European culture. She gathered together important collections of paintings and other art. She founded a new Academy of Sciences as well as a teachers' college. She also encouraged the publication of books and newspapers.

"The Winter Palace was a world of its own. Like a ship floating on the surface of the ocean, it had no real connection with the inhabitants of the deep, beyond that of eating them."

—Alexander Herzen, Russian writer, on St. Petersburg in the time of Catherine the Great, 1858.

Catherine died in 1796, and St. Petersburg entered a period of danger and uncertainty. Her son and heir, Paul, was murdered by his own courtiers in his home, Mikhailovsky Castle, in 1801. Then came the long European war against France and its leader, Napoleon Bonaparte. In August 1812, the French army invaded Russia, only to be forced into retreat in December by hunger and the ferocious winter weather. Czar Alexander I celebrated this Russian victory by commissioning several new buildings for the capital city, including St. Isaac's Cathedral in 1818.

The Road to Revolution

Throughout the nineteenth century, many Russians grew increasingly unhappy with the way their country was being ruled. The Russian royal family had enormous power over its subjects, and people had no voice in government. Most people were desperately poor and uneducated. The Russian army was weak, industry was inefficient, and farming technology had scarcely progressed since the Middle Ages.

▲ *Italian architect Bartolomeo Rastrelli designed the Winter Palace. The Russian royal family lived here from its completion in 1762 until the Revolution of 1917.*

The Winter Palace

Completed in 1762, this was the fourth palace to be built on this site. The vast green and white structure on the banks of the Neva River contains more than one thousand rooms and more than one hundred staircases, and it encloses the central Palace Square. The czars and their families lived here during the long cold winters until the 1880s. The palace forms part of the large complex of buildings that is called the Hermitage.

In December 1825, the people attempted an uprising against Czar Nicholas I. Rebels met for a peaceful demonstration in Senate Square (now known as Decembrists' Square in their honor). Troops shot down hundreds of the demonstrators, and many more were exiled to distant Siberia as punishment.

In 1861, the new czar, Alexander II, abolished the ancient system of serfdom that had forced many peasants to live as slaves. This move, however, meant that thousands of penniless country people surged to the cities to find work in the new factories and mills. St. Petersburg became badly overcrowded, and this led to cramped living conditions, disease, and growing unrest. Alexander II was murdered by a terrorist bomb in 1881. Russia's new ruler was the harsh Alexander III, who limited the freedom of press, gave new powers to the secret police, and did little to help the poor.

By the time Nicholas II became czar in 1894, the revolutionary movement was growing rapidly. Marxists (followers of the communist ideas of Karl Marx) encouraged workers' strikes and protests throughout the

▲ Imperial cavalry charge down on the peaceful protest marchers outside the Winter Palace shown in this painting of "Bloody Sunday," January 22, 1905.

country. St. Petersburg was at the center of many of these protests and has been known ever since as the "Cradle of the Revolution."

In January of 1905, thousands of Russians marched to the Winter Palace to ask Nicholas for reforms. Once again, government soldiers fired on them, killing 70 and wounding 240. The day became known as "Bloody Sunday" and led to more and more violent action by protesters.

In 1914, Russia entered World War I as an opponent of Germany. The name of the city was changed from St. Petersburg (which sounded too Germanic) to Petrograd.

National unrest reached its climax in 1917. The army joined with the rebels, and Nicholas was forced to give up the throne. (He and his family were later killed.) Petrograd became the setting for a new and bloody struggle for power between different

"Two centuries had passed like a dream: Petersburg, standing on the edge of the earth in swamp and wilderness, has day-dreamed of boundless might and glory: palace revolts, assassinations of emperors, triumphs, and bloody executions had flitted past like visions."

—Alexei Tolstoy, Russian historian, 1914

factions. A group called the Bolsheviks ("majority men"), who were led by Vladimir Lenin emerged as the leaders. Moscow replaced Petrograd as the capital of Russia. When Lenin died in 1924, Petrograd was given another new name—Leningrad—in his memory.

The Death of Rasputin

Grigori Rasputin (1869–1916) was an uneducated "holy man" from Siberia, but his healing powers made him the most powerful figure in the court of Czar Nicholas II. Many hated and feared him, and this fuelled public discontent with Nicholas's rule. In 1916, a group of noblemen decided to kill Rasputin. They invited him to visit them, and then fed him poisoned food and wine. When he failed to die, they shot him. Finally, they threw his body (still alive) into the freezing waters of a canal.

▲ The smoking ruins of buildings after a German air raid during the long siege of Leningrad between 1941 and 1944, during World War II.

The Great Siege

The new Communist government of Russia (which was now part of the bigger Union of Soviet Socialist Republics, often called the USSR or the Soviet Union) soon became even more ferocious and repressive than the czars had been. The new leader, Joseph Stalin, started a program to force reforms on farming and industry. Anyone who opposed him was murdered or imprisoned. Millions of people died in these savage purges.

One terror replaced another when World War II began in 1939. The German army invaded Russia in 1941, and Adolf Hitler (Nazi Germany's leader) vowed to destroy Leningrad. The German army surrounded the city that September, shelling the inhabitants and blocking off supplies of

"Living in St. Petersburg is like sleeping in a coffin."

—Osip Mandelstam, Russian poet, at the beginning of Stalin's purges in 1931. He died in a Siberian labor camp in 1938.

food and medicine. The siege lasted for almost nine hundred days, until the Germans retreated in January 1944. During the siege, more than six hundred thousand people died.

The End of the Soviet Union
Soviet troops, alongside U.S. and British allies, played a major part in the eventual defeat of Germany in 1945. This victory gave the Soviet Union control over Poland, Hungary, and many other Eastern European countries. Even though Hitler was defeated, the Soviets still had their own dictator in power. Stalin continued with his campaign of terror against his opponents until his death in 1953. By then, he had extended Soviet domination throughout Eastern Europe, creating an alliance of nations known as the Soviet bloc. The Soviet Union became a superpower, dedicated to spreading communism throughout the world. Fighting the spread of communism stood the world's other superpower, the United States. This conflict, known as the Cold War, never actually led to a direct battle, but it was a war that the Soviet Union eventually lost, mainly for economic reasons.

The Bronze Horseman

One of St. Petersburg's well-known landmarks is the massive statue of Peter the Great on a rearing horse that stands in Decembrists' Square, opposite St. Isaac's Cathedral. Catherine the Great commissioned the sculpture from the sculptor Etienne Falconet, who took twelve years to complete it. Alexander Pushkin wrote a famous poem about the statue called "The Bronze Horseman," and with that name it became a popular symbol of St. Petersburg.

People in the Soviet Union were ruled by fear and repression. Most remained poor and were prevented from learning about the rapidly changing lifestyles in the West. That began to change when Mikhail Gorbachev became Soviet leader in 1985. He started a policy of glasnost ("openness") and began the process of making peace with the United States. Suddenly, Russia was a freer place. Eastern European countries controlled by the Soviets threw out their communist leaders, and by 1991, the Union of Soviet Socialist Republics simply dissolved. Since then, the government of Russia has moved more and more toward privitization and democratic reforms.

A Modern City
Under communism, Leningrad had continued to be the country's cultural center, but its beautiful buildings needed repair. The city could now begin to rebuild.

The citizens elected a reforming leader, and in 1991 voted to restore the old name of St. Petersburg to the city.

    The complete change in politics and society brought enormous problems, however. After decades of money and property being controlled by the government, people were suddenly free to trade for themselves. A few became rich, while many became even poorer than they had been before. Crime flourished, and St. Petersburg soon became famous as a center for organized crime and racketeering.

▲ *Under the gaze of Peter the Great in the background, priests of the Russian Orthodox Church take part in a procession to celebrate the three-hundredth anniversary of the founding of the city.*

Since 2000, conditions have improved. Foreign businesses have invested in the city, roads and other transportation systems have been upgraded, and the city's center has been repaired and cleaned up. In 2003, St. Petersburg celebrated its three-hundredth birthday with festivals and parties.

CHAPTER 2

People of St. Petersburg

The population of St. Petersburg is declining. The number of people living in St. Petersburg dropped by 6 percent between 1989 and 2003. (During this same time period, the population in the Russian city of Moscow increased.) City officials say the reason for the decline is a drop in the birth rate because so many residents of the city are not of childbearing age. In other words, a large number of people living there are under the age of fifteen or over the age of sixty-five.

City of Russians

Native Russians make up the vast majority of the population of St. Petersburg. Native Russians are descendants of the Slavic peoples who lived in this region more than five thousand years ago and gradually inhabited much of Eastern and Central Europe. Many Russians, including those living in St. Petersburg, are also descended from other neighboring peoples, such as the Finns (from Finland) and the Tatars (from central Asia).

◄ *Several couples are married at the same ceremony in the Cathedral of the Transfiguration in St. Petersburg. Group weddings like this are becoming popular in Russia.*

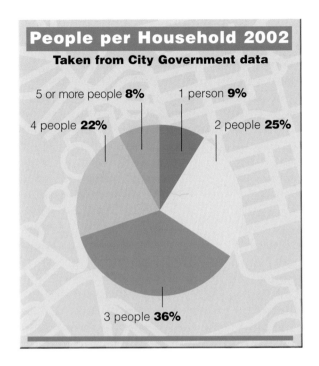

People per Household 2002
Taken from City Government data

5 or more people **8%**

1 person **9%**

4 people **22%**

2 people **25%**

3 people **36%**

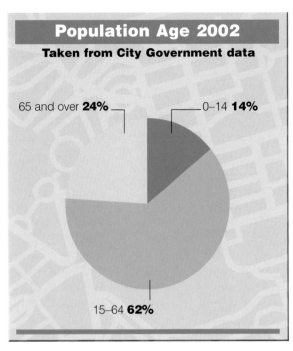

Population Age 2002
Taken from City Government data

65 and over **24%**

0–14 **14%**

15–64 **62%**

▲ *In 2002, the population of St. Petersburg was around 4,596,000. Most lived in small households of between two and four people. Women were more numerous than men, making up 55 percent of the total number. The city's population is much older on average than those in United States, where children up to the age of 14 make up 21 percent of the total. Almost one-fourth of people in St. Petersburg are above the age of 64, compared to 12 percent in the United States.*

Russian is the official language of the country and the most widely spoken language in St. Petersburg. Although it looks and sounds different than English, the Russian and English languages have many words that are similar in sound to each other, such as tri for "three," kofye for "coffee," musey for "museum," and voda for "water." A growing number of Russian people today learn English at school as a second language.

Minority Groups

More than one hundred other national groups live in Russia, and many of these can be found in St. Petersburg's highly mixed population. They include people from neighboring nations that were once a part of the Soviet Union. Among the largest of these groups are Armenians (from southwest Asia), Belorussians (from Belarus, the state between Poland and Russia), Germans, and Jews. Ethnic minorities often speak their own language.

In addition, St. Petersburg has a steadily growing population of temporary residents who come mostly from Western Europe

and North America, the majority of them being students or business travelers. Tourism is also expanding rapidly, bringing thousands of visitors to St. Petersburg every year.

The Orthodox Church

Prince Vladimir adopted the Christian faith for Russia in 988. The nation developed its own form of Christianity—the Russian Orthodox Church—that became a central part of daily life. During the Soviet era, the state was officially atheist (without religion). Christians and followers of other faiths were persecuted, and many places of worship were destroyed.

◄ *The echoing spaces of Russian churches are perfect settings for Orthodox choral music. Regular weekly concerts are held in the Smolny Cathedral in St. Petersburg.*

The Orthodox Easter

Easter is the most important festival of the Russian Orthodox Church. Devout believers take part in the Great Fast (forty days long) before Easter, when they eat no animal products. The main church service begins in the evening of the Easter Saturday. One by one, the candles and other lights are put out until, by midnight, the church is in darkness. At midnight, the candles are again lit, the church bells ring, and worshipers pour out to get ready for their huge Easter feast.

Since the collapse of the Soviet Union in 1991, however, the Russian Orthodox Church has enjoyed a revival. Thousands of people throughout St. Petersburg worship at the city's ten cathedrals and thirty-nine Orthodox churches. The services are usually held twice each day and last for about two hours. The Orthodox faith is traditional, meaning its texts and prayers have changed little since the Middle Ages.

Three major festivals are celebrated in the Orthodox year. The Church uses an old calendar from before the Revolution that is twelve days behind the modern calendar. Christmas Day is celebrated on January 7 and Epiphany on January 19—this marks the day on which Jesus was baptized, and many services take place near rivers and lakes so that believers can be blessed with water. Easter (in March or April) is the climax of the Russian Orthodox calendar.

Other Churches and Faiths

Although the Orthodox Church is by far the most followed faith in the city, nearly every other major religion is represented here as well. A small branch of Orthodox Christians, called the Old Believers, broke away from the main church more than three hundred years ago because they disagreed with changes that were being made. The Old Believers still have two places of worship in St. Petersburg. Other Christian faiths also have their

▲ *Women of St. Petersburg talk together, seated around the traditional samovar, or tea urn.*

churches, including Roman Catholics, Anglicans, Lutherans, Mormons, and the Salvation Army.

St. Petersburg has a steadily growing number of Muslims of the Sunni sect. They worship in the city's only mosque, a building with a tiled dome and minarets. Jews have been a part of St. Petersburg's life since its founding, and today there are two synagogues, including the ornate Great Choral Synagogue. There is also a Jewish cemetery for Bloody Sunday victims. Buddhists worship at Kuntsechoinei Datsan Temple.

Buying Food

Since the end of the Soviet era, trade has become freer, and a greater variety of food has become available in Russian cities. St. Petersburg has plenty of street markets buzzing with life and offering a huge variety of produce, including fruit, vegetables, honey, cheese, and other fresh foods. And the number of western-like supermarkets is growing.

Residents of St. Petersburg find it hard to resist the many street vendors selling snacks. Shawarma (hot sandwiches) stands are near the entrances to most metro (subway) stations, and the wider streets and squares contain burger and hot dog stands. Other food vendors offer everything from pastries and pancakes to doughnuts and ice cream.

Mealtimes

Russian cooking reflects the enormous size of the country. Its many different regions and cultures have each contributed dishes and influences. Among them are spicy shashlyk (lamb kebabs) from Georgia, pelmeny (meat dumplings in stew) from Siberia, and chicken Kiev (chicken breasts filled with garlic butter) from Ukraine—all of which are enjoyed in St. Petersburg.

Breakfast food is simple—usually sweetened, weak tea served alongside either porridge and homemade jam or cold meat, boiled eggs, and bread. Lunch was once considered the most important meal in Russia, lasting at least two hours in the middle of the day. Now the people of St. Petersburg (and other cities in Russia) are beginning to follow the customs of the United States and Western Europe, with much shorter lunches—a plain soup or salad followed by meat or fish.

The evening meal is now the day's main meal in many households. It begins with an array of zakuski (appetizers), which might include smoked fish, pickled cucumbers, and rye bread. Appetizers might be followed by borscht (beet soup) and caviar (the roe, or eggs, of the sturgeon fish). The main course often consist of meat in a thick sauce. Dessert might be pastries, tarts, or ice cream.

Drinking

Russians drink a lot of tea, made very strong in a pot or samovar, which is a special Russian tea urn with a spigot, and then diluted in the cup with hot water or, occasionally, with milk. Many also drink teas made from dried herbs and sweetened with homemade jelly. Russians also drink other nonalcoholic beverages including mineral water from natural springs and fruit juices.

Vodka is also widely consumed in Russia. Distilled from grain and sometimes flavored with fruits, spices, or herbs, vodka is strong (at least 40 percent alcohol) and the cause of a high level of health problems, drunkenness, and other personal and societal problems. Other alcoholic beverages are available to the people of St. Petersburg, including wines made from grapes grown in southern Russia and a weak beer called kvass made from rye bread.

CHAPTER 3

Living in St. Petersburg

Everyday life in Russia and St. Petersburg was transformed by the collapse of the Soviet Union in 1991. Instead of rigid government control of everything from food and clothing to travel and industry, there was freedom. Prices for goods shot up, and crime increased. A few people became very wealthy, but most incomes stayed very low. In recent years, however, conditions have improved for citizens of St. Petersburg. The economy has stabilized, and the city's infrastructure (buildings and roads) is being repaired or replaced.

Apartments

St. Petersburg is beautiful to look at, but for many it is a harsh place in which to live. This is partly due to a shortage of good and affordable housing in the city. As many as three hundred thousand residents still live in big communal apartments, called *kommunalki*, that they rent from the city council.

These buildings were once mansions that were seized by the government after the 1917 Revolution and used to house as many families as possible. Today, the overcrowded

◄ *Frequent snow is a fact of life for residents in St. Petersburg. Here, pedestrians walk through sleet over the Anichkov Bridge.*

▲ *Typical high-rise, suburban apartment buildings made of concrete loom over a tram, taking commuters to work in the city center.*

conditions have changed very little. Most families in a kommunalki live and sleep in a single room, cook in the building's shared kitchen, and line up to use the building's only bathroom. There is little privacy. Russian president Vladimir Putin grew up in St. Petersburg in a kommunalki like the one described here.

St. Petersburg has been slower than other cities in Russia (such as Moscow) to get rid of its old-fashioned, rundown apartment buildings. Now, however, there is a push to sell the buildings and make the multiple tenants move out. Buyers of the kommunalki are often wealthy families who take over the entire building and live there, or they are developers who refurbish the buildings and rent them out. As a result, housing in St. Petersburg has become limited and very expensive.

Suburbs and Palaces

St. Petersburg's suburbs are expanding as single-family homes and apartment buildings are erected in an attempt to relieve the desperate shortage of housing in the city. New dwellings are going up alongside complexes that were completed during the 1970s and 1980s and that are often unattractive and cheaply built. Tenants from the old kommunalki in the city can find new homes in these areas.

▲ Shoppers choose from a display of pastries and breads at a bakery in Pazzazh, the 590-foot–(180-m-) long gallery of shops on Nevsky Prospect.

Beyond the suburbs lie the areas where the very wealthiest of people live. The most amazing of these is a brand-new development near the Lahti Bay on the Gulf of Finland. Here, the super-rich can buy houses that are miniature versions of famous palaces. Among the fifty houses being completed are replicas of the city's own Petrodvorets (Peter the Great's summer palace to the west of St. Petersburg) and the famous Versailles Palace in France.

Shops and Shopping

Nevsky Prospect is one of the best-known streets in all of Russia. Massive department stores offer everything from clothing to food. Alongside the shops and stores are many hotels, places of worship, and entertainment venues. During the Soviet

"The quality of life has significantly increased and the city has begun to look far better."

—Alexandre Kourotchkin and Irina Kurachenkova in "Elements of Good Governance in St. Petersburg," 2003.

Living with Ice and Snow

Temperatures in the winter months in St. Petersburg can fall as low as 5° F (-15° C). Snow and ice cover the ground, and the wind from the Gulf of Finland is bitingly cold. Besides the cold and the slippery ground, there is also danger from falling icicles from tall buildings during warmer spells. The Neva River (above) freezes over every winter, but it is a tradition for some to swim in the river all winter long through a hole cut in the ice.

era, shops in the city were mostly state-owned; they usually looked dull and were badly stocked. Today, however, many stores display goods imported from abroad, and some are owned by foreign corporations. The competition and wider choice has made shopping more exciting for residents and visitors.

Travel in the City

With a major seaport, an international airport, four large railroad stations,

▲ Several new metro stations have been built to serve the city's suburbs. This one is on Grazdansky Prospect.

and fifteen highways, St. Petersburg is the largest transportation center in Russia. The massive Seaport Terminal on the edge of the city contains docks for handling timber and other cargoes, ship repair yards, and a passenger ship terminal 1 mile (1.6 km) long. Liners and ferries arrive here from Scandinavia and other western ports, and a mooring area is available for riverboats.

Pulkovo Airport lies 9 miles (15 km) south of the city. It has two passenger terminals (one for domestic flights and one for international flights) as well as a large cargo handling area. The main railroad stations are named after their destinations—Moscow, Finland (which connects with Helsinki), Warsaw (in Poland), and Vitebsk (in Belarus). The metro, or subway, runs four underground lines that connect the city outskirts with its center. This provides a safe and efficient service and is the world's deepest underground rail system.

Road traffic in St. Petersburg is heavy on weekdays, especially during the morning

Railway to Revolution

One of St. Petersburg's most famous landmarks is a railway station. Finland Station, on the Neva River, holds a proud place in Russian history. It was here that Vladimir Lenin arrived at the height of the Revolution in 1917 on his return from exile in Switzerland. He went on to become the most powerful and influential figure in the early years of communist rule.

and evening rush hours, but people can choose to use public transportation. Buses are the best way of reaching the city outskirts, while trams and trolleys (electric buses) crisscross the central area. The fifteen hundred taxis that operate in the city are a mixture of official yellow vehicles and cars owned by private companies or individuals.

Crime and Pollution

In spite of heavy traffic and nearby industrial zones, St. Petersburg has little problem with smoke, fumes, and other forms of air pollution because it lies near the sea with its strong winds that carry the pollution away and keep the atmosphere fairly clean. A greater threat comes from the aging nuclear power station to the west of the city. The power station is now more than twenty-five years old and needs constant repair and maintenance to prevent it from leaking dangerous radiation.

Crime is another major problem for modern St. Petersburg. Crime ranges from pickpockets to car thieves to illegal arms sales to drug trafficking. Criminal organizations also operate large-scale "protection" rackets. When a local business starts to make a profit, the racketeers move in and demand regular payments of money in exchange for "protecting" the company from violence or other threats.

The Banya

A trip to the public *banya*, or bathhouse, is a favorite part of the week for many people in St. Petersburg. Banyas throughout the city accommodate men and women in separate sections. The bathers take off all their clothes, wrap themselves in sheets, and go to the dry sauna room. Here the heat is strong and dry to encourage sweating. Then bathers move to the steam room where water is thrown onto hot rocks to create steam. Sometimes, bathers "beat" each other lightly with bunches of birch twigs in an attempt to remove toxins from the body. This action sounds violent, but it is not. Next comes a plunge into cold water. This whole process can be repeated to last as long as two hours. People leave the banya feeling clean and relaxed.

Schools and Colleges

Many Russian children start school young, as early as age three for preschool classes. Between the ages of six and fifteen, children must attend what is called "basic" school,

where they are given a basic and wide-ranging education. Some students then go on to high school, where they study at least twelve subjects and take examinations to gain their Certificate of Secondary General Education. Others go to technical schools and learn a specific trade or profession.

▲ A group of young Russian sailors celebrate their graduation from college. There are twenty-two military academies in St. Petersburg.

The style of teaching in Russian schools is still very traditional, with an emphasis on learning rules, dates, math tables, and a

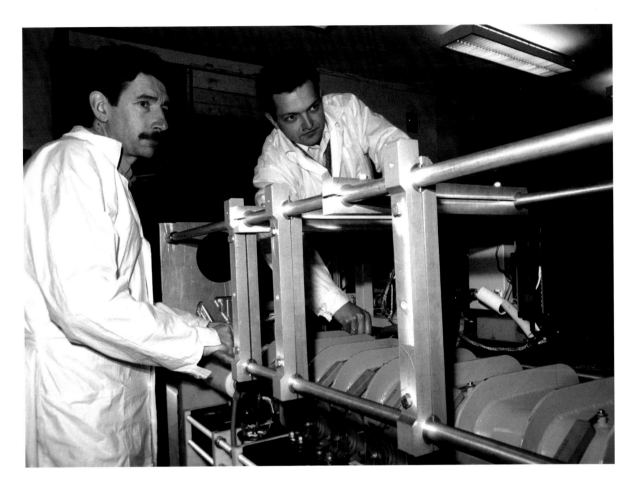

▲ *Russian students work in the laser laboratory at the Baltic State Technical University, an engineering college that specializes in rocket science.*

foreign language (usually English). Children as young as three begin to learn through poems, games, and songs. At six years of age, children start their more formal education. The traditional methods make certain that an exceptionally high proportion of Russian children (more than 95 percent) can read and write.

Students who succeed in gaining their secondary certificate can apply to go on to higher education and study for a degree— usually for four years. St. Petersburg State University is one of the most highly regarded post-secondary schools in Russia, while the St. Petersburg Technical University specializes in the study of engineering and computer technology.

"It is not necessary to know all the facts. We try to give children the chance to think and be creative."

—Vladimir Filippov, Russian Education Minister, on changing attitudes to teaching, 2004

CHAPTER 4

St. Petersburg at Work

One of the most successful areas in modern Russia, St. Petersburg is the second most important center for industry and finance after Moscow, and its position on the Gulf of Finland makes it a vital outlet for sea transportation to the West. Like other parts of the country, however, it is still trying to make up for decades of stagnation under Soviet rule, which can be seen clearly in the shortage of skilled and specially trained workers. A shortage of skilled labor means that many companies have a hard time finding suitable employees.

Industry

Several factors have made St. Petersburg a major industrial city. One is its port facilities and easy access to the Baltic Sea and Europe. Another is the rich supply of natural resources in the region, including bauxite (for manufacturing aluminum), timber, and iron ore. Today, the area is responsible for more than 3 percent of all Russian manufactured goods.

◀ *Many Russians now drink beer as a healthier alternative to the much stronger vodka. As a result, production in breweries, such as the Baltika in St. Petersburg, has soared.*

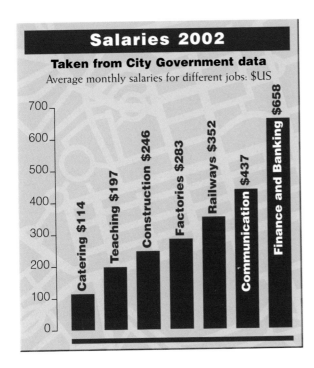

Salaries 2002

Taken from City Government data
Average monthly salaries for different jobs: $US

- Catering $114
- Teaching $197
- Construction $246
- Factories $283
- Railways $352
- Communication $437
- Finance and Banking $658

◄ *Financial and business services are growing in St. Petersburg and provide the best paid jobs in the city. Workers in these areas earn on average more than three times the salary of teachers and more than twice the wages of factory workers.*

Factories such as the Kirov Plant and Leningrad Metal Works produce heavy machinery, and the many shipyards, such as Baltiysky Zavod and Almaz, manufacture all types of sea vessels, from yachts to nuclear-powered icebreakers. St. Petersburg boasts Russia's biggest beer brewery (Baltika) as well as many other food-processing plants. Local timber is used to make paper and furniture, and flax and other local crops are made into a variety of textiles.

Imports and Exports
For more than seventy years, the government controlled the economy of Russia, and most private business ideas were stifled. This had a particularly negative effect on the trade of importing and exporting goods. Since the end of Soviet rule, however, the new freedom has encouraged Russians to set up international trading companies, and many foreign corporations have established branches in Russian cities including St. Petersburg. Some of St. Petersburg's imports include foods, household products, medicines, and chemicals. Major exports include the industrial products already mentioned as well as computer and other electrical goods.

Breaking the Ice

Every winter, St. Petersburg's harbor freezes over. This is partly because the water here is shallow and the sea has a low salt content (which means it freezes at a higher temperature than very salty water). It is vital that the dock area is kept open for shipping. Boats called icebreakers plow up and down every day, using their powerful engines and specially strengthened hulls to crack the ice and clear wide channels.

"We have gone from total protection to total exposure. They throw us off a cliff and say 'Fly!' "

—St. Petersburg official describing the shock of economic freedom after the end of the Soviet Union.

▲ St. Petersburg has been a major academic center for more than two centuries, providing opportunities for many teachers and researchers. This woman works at an institute studying new techniques in plant growth and the conservation of seeds.

Finance and Services

Financial and business services form a big part of St. Petersburg's economy, and the city now has the country's second-largest money market after Moscow. The city has its own stock exchange, currency exchange, and a wide range of commercial banks and other financial institutions. These include the Baltiyskiy Bank and Menatep St. Petersburg that cover all sectors of finance business, from banking to insurance.

Dramatic growth has occurred in companies that provide services for industry and the community. Among the most important of these are the recruitment and training agencies, which are vital in helping to find enough people to work at the newly created jobs in the rapidly expanding economy. In May 2004, for example, more than sixty-eight thousand job vacancies existed in St. Petersburg—many of them needing skilled workers. The city is now the center for industrial and management training in northwest Russia.

Preserving the Past

Restoring Catherine the Great's private retreat, the Chinese Palace at Lomonosov (Oranienbaum), is a big challenge. Though damp and musty, its ornate interior of wood and gold leaf has barely been touched since the eighteenth century. Much of the decoration is still held together with the original glue—made from vodka and fish bones. A sudden drying-out would ruin this, so conservationists decided to keep it at a steady level of dampness to ensure that the glue (and the other antique materials) would not be disturbed. So far, this bold experiment has worked.

Tourism and the Media

St. Petersburg stands eighth in the list of top tourist towns in the world. Every year, more than 2.6 million foreigners visit the city, as well as 800,000 people from other parts of the Russian Federation. Tourism brings in a great deal of money and employs a large sector of the population, who operate the

▼ *The German Nazi invaders stripped many treasures from the region, including the lovely décor of the Amber Room at the Catherine Palace in Tsarskoe Selo. The Amber room is now being carefully restored by skilled craftspeople, seen here working with amber.*

Russian Ark

The beautiful palaces and streets of St. Petersburg have made it a popular setting for films and TV programs. The film Russian Ark *(2003) re-created a nineteenth-century ball inside the Hermitage, with a cast of many hundreds. The director was only allowed a short time for his filming, so he completed it in just one shot—which lasted for 90 minutes. A single camera moved through the maze of passages and rooms in the palace capturing many different scenes. One mistake and the whole project would have been ruined.*

▶ *Two policemen examine a man's identity and search his pockets. The police often give fines on the spot for minor offenses.*

many restaurants, guesthouses, souvenir shops, major hotels, and visitor complexes.

One sign of the city's popularity with foreigners is the three English-language newspapers and magazines published here especially for them. Russians can choose to read many national papers, including *Izvestia, Kommersant,* and the government daily *Rossiyskaya Gazeta.* The press became officially free of state control in the early 1990s, but in recent years, several journalists have been murdered in revenge for their investigations into corruption and other high-level crime. This means that some papers now don't dare to criticize big business or the government.

St. Petersburg has four television stations, including the national channel Rossiya and TV-Petersburg, as well as several cable channels serving local districts. These broadcast news, movies, game shows, and sports, plus foreign soap operas dubbed into Russian. Two local radio stations concentrate on news, and a large number of music stations play a variety of popular music.

Governing St. Petersburg

The leader of St. Petersburg is called governor rather than mayor (the title was changed in 1996). The governor controls the city through three major assemblies. The Legislative Assembly (or Parliament) consists of fifty deputies; it passes local laws and decides on matters such as taxes and the city budget. The City Administration does the daily work of running municipal affairs, and the Court Authority runs the justice system.

Several committees operate within the administration, covering every aspect of city business, from road improvements and public housing repairs to tourism, culture, and sports. St. Petersburg also is divided into more than one hundred district "units," each with its own council that decides on local issues. Elections to appoint the governor, parliamentary deputies, committee members, and local councilors are held every four years.

Law and Order

Three kinds of police work in the city. The traffic police are responsible for checking

licenses and other documents and have the power to stop drivers. Another of their duties is to ease the flow of traffic and catch people who drive dangerously.

Beat officers are usually armed and wear dark blue uniforms. They can stop and question people they suspect of committing offenses—however small—and have the power to impose fines on the spot. St. Petersburg now has a third police force, specially formed to tackle the increase in organized crime.

CHAPTER 5

St. Petersburg at Play

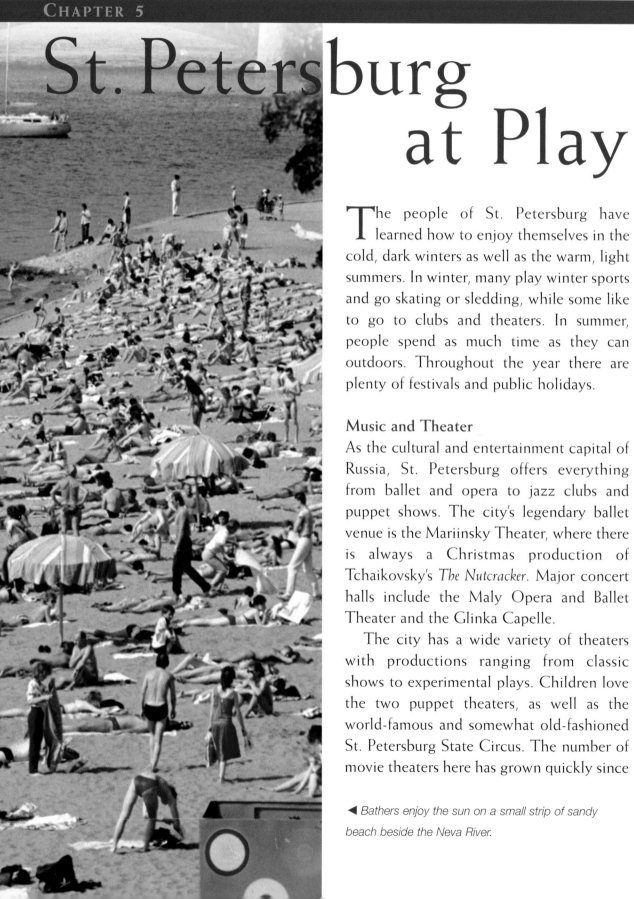

The people of St. Petersburg have learned how to enjoy themselves in the cold, dark winters as well as the warm, light summers. In winter, many play winter sports and go skating or sledding, while some like to go to clubs and theaters. In summer, people spend as much time as they can outdoors. Throughout the year there are plenty of festivals and public holidays.

Music and Theater

As the cultural and entertainment capital of Russia, St. Petersburg offers everything from ballet and opera to jazz clubs and puppet shows. The city's legendary ballet venue is the Mariinsky Theater, where there is always a Christmas production of Tchaikovsky's *The Nutcracker*. Major concert halls include the Maly Opera and Ballet Theater and the Glinka Capelle.

The city has a wide variety of theaters with productions ranging from classic shows to experimental plays. Children love the two puppet theaters, as well as the world-famous and somewhat old-fashioned St. Petersburg State Circus. The number of movie theaters here has grown quickly since

◄ *Bathers enjoy the sun on a small strip of sandy beach beside the Neva River.*

Soviet times, and people can see the latest Hollywood films dubbed into Russian.

Nightlife

The streets are often full of people all evening and often far into the early morning hours. Many just talk and walk, but there is also a lively nightclub and disco scene, which has grown rapidly since the 1990s. Clubs, from small cellar bars to large halls with multiple dance floors, cater to every taste.

Open Spaces

The center of St. Petersburg, with its flat setting and wide streets, has a spacious feel, and many parks, squares, and other open areas are open to the public, including Admiralty Gardens and Yelagin Island, with its palace, peaceful woodland, and graveled paths. The city has a few beaches, from the small beach next to the Peter and Paul Fortress to the wide shores of the Gulf of Finland.

Many families have small country cottages called dachas away from the city, where they often spend the summer weekends. Here they may garden, walk, fish, or gather wild fruits and mushrooms.

Festivals throughout the Year

Russians throw themselves into their festivals and public holidays with great pride and enthusiasm. St. Petersburg, with its dramatic history and inviting setting, hosts many festivals. Some celebrate the change of seasons, such as the Goodbye Russian Winter festival that features folk music and sleigh rides. Others recall great moments in history, such as Victory Day on May 9 that commemorates the German surrender in 1945. The founding of the city itself is remembered on May 27 and is called City Day.

Great Creators

Alexander Pushkin (1799–1837)

Though born in Moscow, Pushkin spent many years in St. Petersburg as a young man. He is still Russia's best-loved poet, and many Russians know by heart passages from his great verse novel Eugene Onegin.

Fyodor Dostoyevsky (1821–1881)

No one has described the harsh life of St. Petersburg's slums better than Dostoyevsky. The settings of his most famous novel Crime and Punishment *can still be seen, and his home on Kuznechny Pereulok is now a museum.*

Peter Ilyich Tchaikovsky (1840–1893)

Tchaikovsky was a music student in St. Petersburg who developed a deep interest in Russian folk tunes. He was the first Russian composer to gain fame in Western Europe, especially with the ballets Swan Lake *and* Sleeping Beauty.

Anna Akhmatova (1889–1966)

Another of Russia's great poets, Akhmatova spent most of her life in St. Petersburg, even though many of her family and friends were imprisoned or killed. Stalin banned much of her later work for not being "communist" enough.

Music and ballet events play a central part in the city's calendar. The Mariinsky Ballet Festival takes place in February, the Kuryokhin Music Festival in April, the Spring Music Festival in May, and a series of Christmas concerts in December. There are also major jazz festivals in March and November, and a Baltic Theater Festival in October, with performances in theaters and on the streets.

▲ The Kirov Ballet, one of the best-loved companies in the world, performs at the Mariinsky Theater.

Watching and Playing Sports

Under Soviet rule, Russians were encouraged to do well in sports, so several sports complexes stand from that era, with swimming pools, gyms, and running tracks. St. Petersburg's best-known soccer team is FC Zenit (Zenith), and they play at

▲ *Pavel Mares (right) of FC Zenit St. Petersburg battles for the ball in a soccer match against Spanish team Sevilla in 2004.*

White Nights

The last days of June are St. Petersburg's midsummer, when days are so long that there is only a short period of darkness. These are called the "White Nights," and they are a time of 24-hour celebrations when many people go to bed very late—if at all. Special events include festivals of classical, jazz, and rock music.

Cold winters give people a chance to enjoy many different sports, such as sledding, ice fishing, and cross-country skiing. Skating on frozen ponds and rivers is popular, and year-round skating rinks are located at the Kirov Stadium and the Yubileiny Sports Palace. Ice hockey is also widely played.

Out of Town

The countryside around the city is very flat, but it contains plenty of fine and fascinating places to visit. St. Petersburgers are very proud of their natural heritage, which includes large lakes, islands, sand caves, and pine forests (the home of bears, wild boar, and birds of prey). The area also boasts a range of imperial palaces, parks, and picturesque villages, where many of the historic buildings are now being restored after years of neglect or damage during World War II.

To the southeast is Novgorod, one of the oldest towns in the region, which was founded more than eleven hundred years ago. Novgorod's medieval Cathedral of

Petrovsky Stadium. It was here that the city hosted the Goodwill Games in 1994. Another major sporting event is the St. Petersburg Open Tennis tournament, which attracts world-class players each year.

The Treasures of the Hermitage

The Hermitage (above) on the banks of the Neva River is one of the most celebrated art museums in the world today. More than three million visitors come here every year to see the astonishing collection of paintings, sculptures, jewelry, china, and coins from all periods and civilizations. One whole floor houses objects from prehistoric Russia, as well as from ancient Egypt, Greece, and Rome. Elsewhere there are displays of work by some of the greatest artists in history, most notably Rembrandt, Leonardo da Vinci, Caravaggio, Van Gogh, and Matisse.

St. Sophia, with its beautiful bronze doors and icons, has become a place of pilgrimage for Orthodox Christians in post-Soviet Russia. Vyborg, lying northwest on the road to Helsinki, is another ancient settlement, with a castle dramatically built on a rock just off the coast.

Russia's emperors built several huge estates near St. Petersburg. The biggest is Petrodvorets (also known as Peterhof), which was established by Peter the Great

▲ *Peter the Great had several small palaces built in the huge grounds of the Petrodvorets, or Peterhof. The Marly Palace (on the left) sits beside the waters of the Gulf of Finland.*

overlooking the Baltic on the coast to the west. With its magnificent palace and famous Grand Cascade (a massive system of water features containing 140 fountains) this is a favorite destination for a day out from the city.

Equally famous is Tsarskoe Selo (also called Pushkin, in honor of the poet), to the south of St. Petersburg. Created by the Empresses Elizabeth and Catherine the Great, this features a vast palace with a frontage that is more than 1,000 feet (300 meters) long, decorated with pillars, statues, balconies, and exquisitely carved windows. Around the palace is a massive park, with ponds, pavilions, and even a Turkish bathhouse.

CHAPTER 6

Looking Forward

No Russian city has gained more in the freedom of the post-Soviet era than St. Petersburg. Its fame and beauty have drawn huge numbers of tourists and other visitors, while its dock facilities and transportation advantages have attracted investors and foreign businesses. Even its restored name has brought back a romantic glow to the city. With an ever-growing amount of wealth pouring in and plans being developed for expansion and restoration, its future looks bright.

The Putin Factor

One reason for the city's prosperity is the Russian president, Vladimir Putin. Born in St. Petersburg, he became its deputy mayor in 1994. Since he was elected as president in 2000 (and again in 2004), Putin has promised that his hometown will regain its position not only as cultural capital but also as a political center.

The full effect of this promise remains to be seen in years to come. Already the president has transferred a fund of $500 million from Moscow to St. Petersburg. He has also hosted important meetings there with foreign leaders. He is determined that the Konstantinovsky Palace will be used for

◀ *U.S. President George W. Bush* (right) *appears on the balcony of the Petrodvorets Palace as a guest of Russian President Vladimir Putin* (left).

▲ *Many of the city's great historic monuments have been restored in recent years. Here, the repaired Alexander Column in Dvortsovaya Square is unveiled in 2003.*

state receptions and that some government departments will be moved from Moscow to St. Petersburg. All of this has caused jealousy in Moscow and other major towns, but it has brought a renewed sense of pride and optimism to the people of St. Petersburg.

The city's image as a glittering showpiece has been enhanced by a long-term program of restoration and repair to the great buildings and other landmarks. The money for this comes partly from central government and partly from sponsors at home and abroad.

Power Position

St. Petersburg's location on the Baltic still makes it Russia's "Window on the West," as it was when it was founded in 1703. But "the West" now includes the European Union (EU), an organization of nations that work together in economic and other areas. The growing strength of the EU gives St. Petersburg—as the nearest Russian city—a new importance in the affairs of the continent.

"St. Petersburg has huge potential in the areas of education, culture, technology, industry, and tourism."

—Alexandre Kourotchkin and Irina Kurachenkova in "Elements of Good Governance in St. Petersburg," 2003.

Time Line

1689 Peter the Great becomes czar of Russia.

1700–1721 Peter goes to war with Sweden to gain access to the Baltic Sea.

1703 Peter drives the Swedes from the mouth of the Neva River and establishes St. Petersburg.

1709 A major victory over Sweden at Poltava secures the region for Russia.

1712 St. Petersburg becomes Russia's new capital city, and the royal court is established there.

1725 Peter the Great dies, and the court moves back to Moscow.

1741 Elizabeth becomes Russia's new ruler, and the court returns to St. Petersburg.

1762–1796 Catherine the Great rules Russia.

1762 The Winter Palace is completed.

1812 The French army invades Russia but is forced to retreat in winter.

1818 Alexander I celebrates the defeat of France by commissioning St. Isaac's Cathedral and other buildings.

1825 The Decembrists rebel against Alexander's rule.

1833 Alexander Pushkin publishes his poem "The Bronze Horseman."

1861 Czar Alexander II abolishes serfdom.

1881 Alexander II is assassinated.

1894 Nicholas II becomes czar of Russia.

1905 Revolution breaks out briefly after "Bloody Sunday" shootings outside the Winter Palace.

1914–1918 Russia fights on the side of the Allies in World War I.

1914 St. Peterburg's name is changed to Petrograd.

1916 Rasputin is murdered by a group of noblemen.

1917 Revolution breaks out again. Vladimir Lenin returns from exile to St. Petersburg and becomes Russia's new leader.

1924 Lenin dies, and St. Petersburg is renamed Leningrad in his honor.

1924 Joseph Stalin becomes leader of Soviet Russia.

1928–1929 Stalin purges the urban areas to get rid of intellectuals and other rivals.

1939–1945 Russia fights on the side of the Allies in World War II.

1941 The German army invades Russia and begins its siege of Leningrad.

1944 The siege is lifted after nearly nine hundred days, and the German army retreats.

1953 Stalin dies.

1985 Mikhail Gorbachev becomes Soviet leader and introduces new policies of glasnost.

1991 The Soviet Union is dissolved and the Russian Federation formed.

1991 Leningrad becomes St. Petersburg again.

1998 Russia experiences a financial crisis.

2000 Vladimir Putin is elected president of Russia.

2003 St. Petersburg celebrates its three-hundredth birthday.

2004 Putin is reelected president.

Glossary

bauxite the mixture of minerals and impurities that is found in the ground and processed to make aluminum.

Bolsheviks a Russian word for "majority men," describing members of the left-wing socialist group led by Lenin during the Russian Revolution.

budget a detailed plan for income and spending during a given period.

classical a style of architecture that copies the designs and techniques of ancient Greece and Rome.

commissioned hired to produce a piece of work.

communal something that is shared by everyone in a group or community.

communism a system of government that aims to create a classless society where everyone is equal; businesses are run by the state for the good of the people, and all property is communally owned.

communist a person who believes in communism.

courtiers members of a royal court.

dictator a ruler who has absolute control over the government.

factions groups within a group who have different interests and agendas.

federation a group of states or societies that have joined together.

flax a plant from which fibers are used for making cloth.

Germanic relating to or coming from the area that is modern-day Germany.

minaret a tall tower on a mosque; a prayer leader often stands in a minaret to call Muslims to prayer.

nuclear power station a structure in which electricity is generated through energy released in a nuclear reaction.

organized crime criminal activities, including theft, gambling, prostitution, and racketeering, committed by formally organized groups.

patron saint a saint who is supposed to protect a place or organization and to whom that place or organization is dedicated.

purges acts of getting rid of people who are hated or not wanted.

racketeering a system of obtaining money through scare tactics and intimidation.

radiation the invisible waves or particles given off by a nuclear reaction that can cause sickness and death.

serfdom a system in which some are bound by law to work for (and be controlled by) a lord or master of the land.

Soviet local and national governing councils of a communist country.

Soviet Union the Union of Soviet Socialist Republics—a nation made up of Russia, Ukraine, and other communist states in Eastern Europe and Asia between 1917 and 1991.

stagnation lack of movement or growth.

suburb a community or development on the edge of a city.

superpower a very strong and influential nation that can force its will upon other nations.

USSR *see* Soviet Union

Further Information

Books

Bjornlund, Britta. *The Russian Revolution* People at the Center of (series). Blackbirch, 2004.

Hirtz, Martin. *Russia* True Books (series). Children's Press, 2004.

Kent, Deborah. *St. Petersburg* Cities of the World (series). Children's Press, 1997.

Kokker, Steve and Nick Selby. *Lonely Planet: St. Petersburg*. Lonely Planet, 2005.

Petrovna, Yevgenia. *St. Petersburg: A Portrait of the City and Its Citizens*. Palace Editions, 2005.

Phillips, Catherine, Christopher and Melanie Rice. *Eyewitness Travel Guides: St. Petersburg*. Dorling Kindersley, 2001.

Rogers, Stillman. *Russia* Enchantment of the World (series). Children's Press, 2002.

Streissguth, Tom. *Vladimir Putin: Biography*. Lerner, 2005.

Torchinsky, Oleg. *Russia* Cultures of the World (series). Benchmark, 2005.

Websites

www.hermitagemuseum.org
Discover details about the art treasures in the Hermitage.

www.infoservices.com/stpete
Explore a full directory of services, sites, and useful addresses in St. Petersburg.

www.omniglot.com/writing /cyrillic
See the complete Russian alphabet as it was in the tenth century and in subsequent centuries as it changed.

www.petersburg-russia.com
Access a city guide with a lot of travel information.

www.russia.com
Visit a national site full of news and travel information.

www.saint-petersburg.com
Enjoy a travel and event guide, featuring a video of the city and a web cam.

www.sptimes.ru
Read a daily online English-language newspaper about the city.

Index